Contact me

Instagram

@bite2breakskin

**follow me for more artwork or send me a
direct message if you need to get in touch**

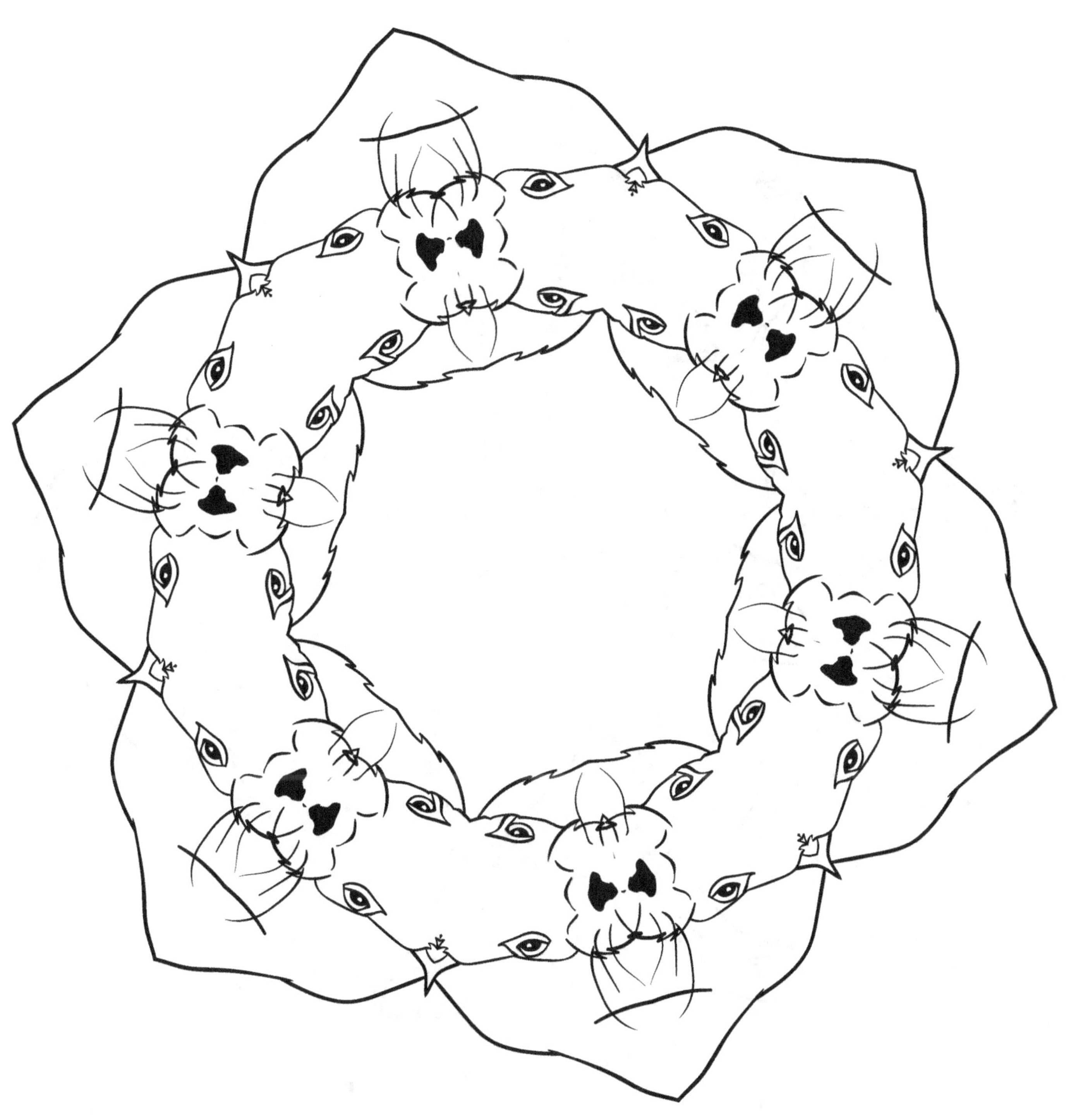

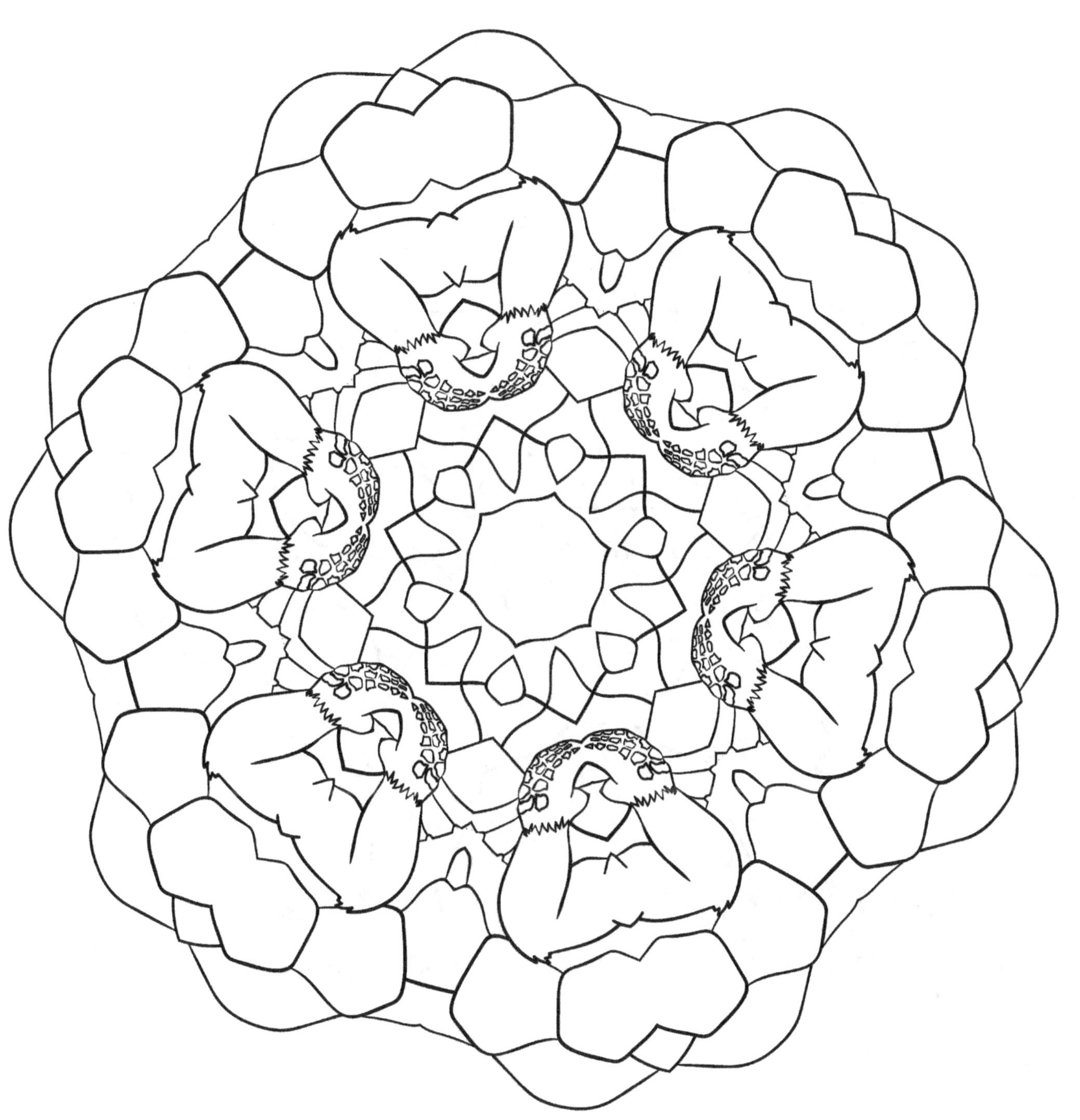

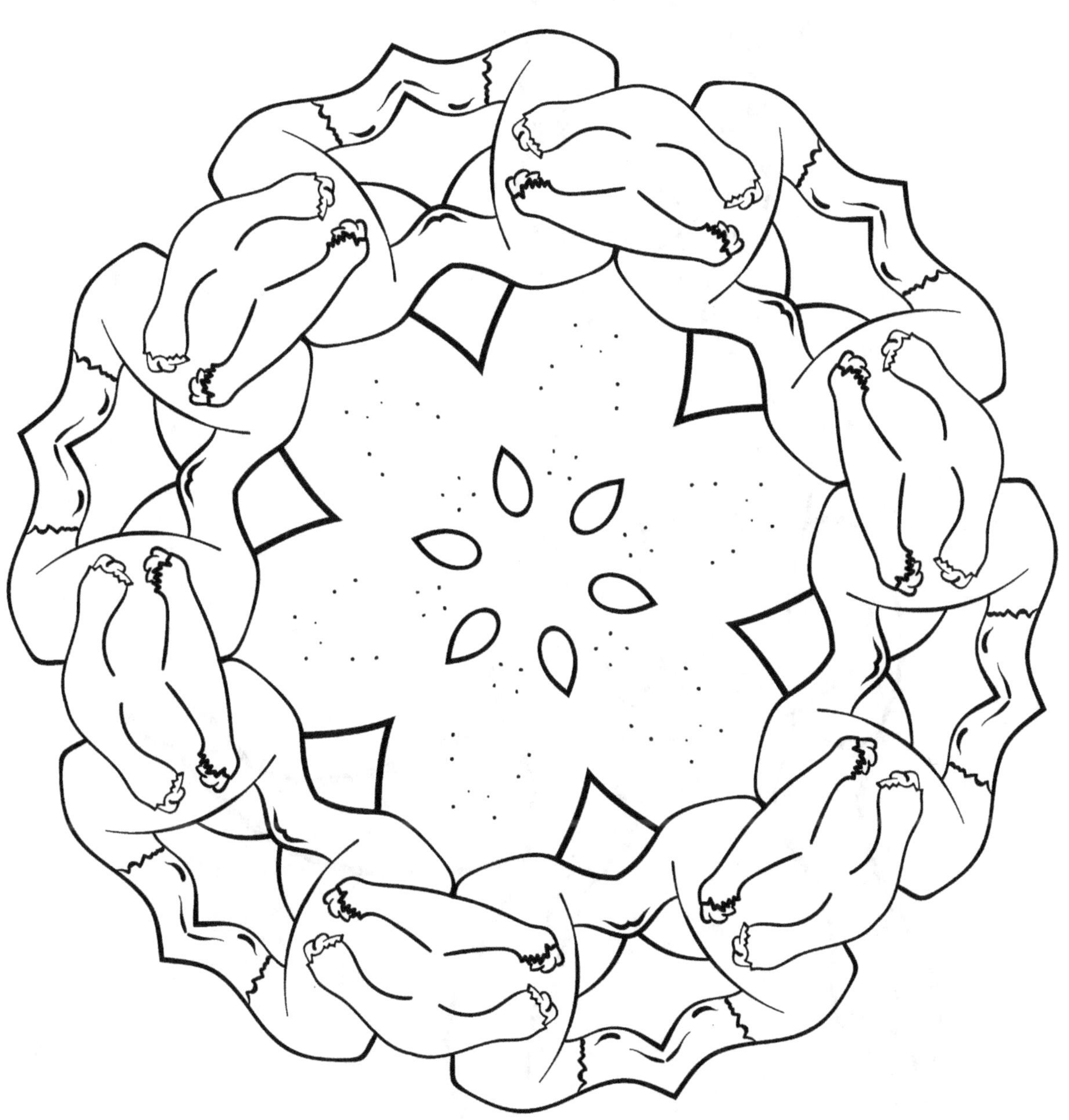

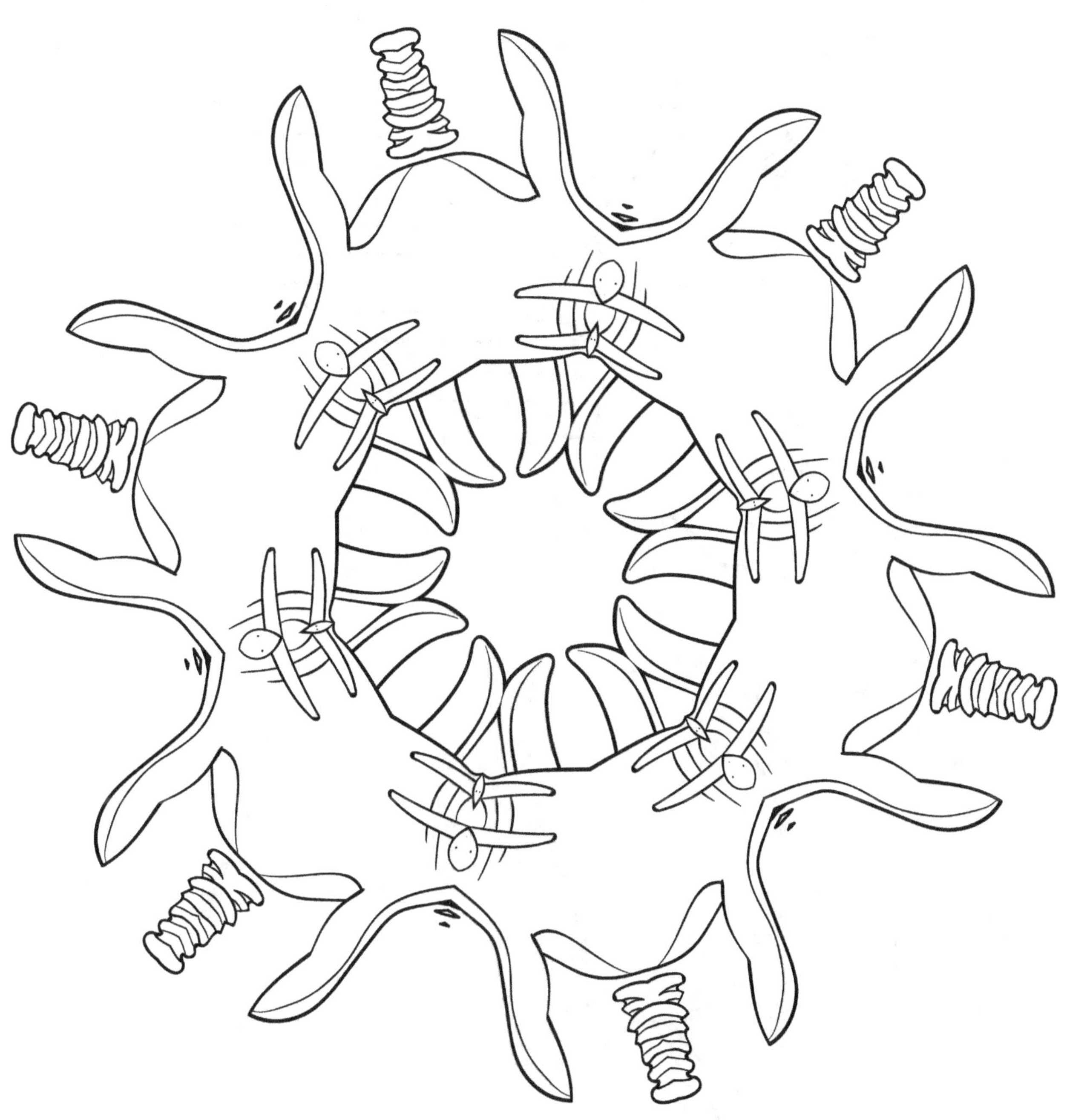

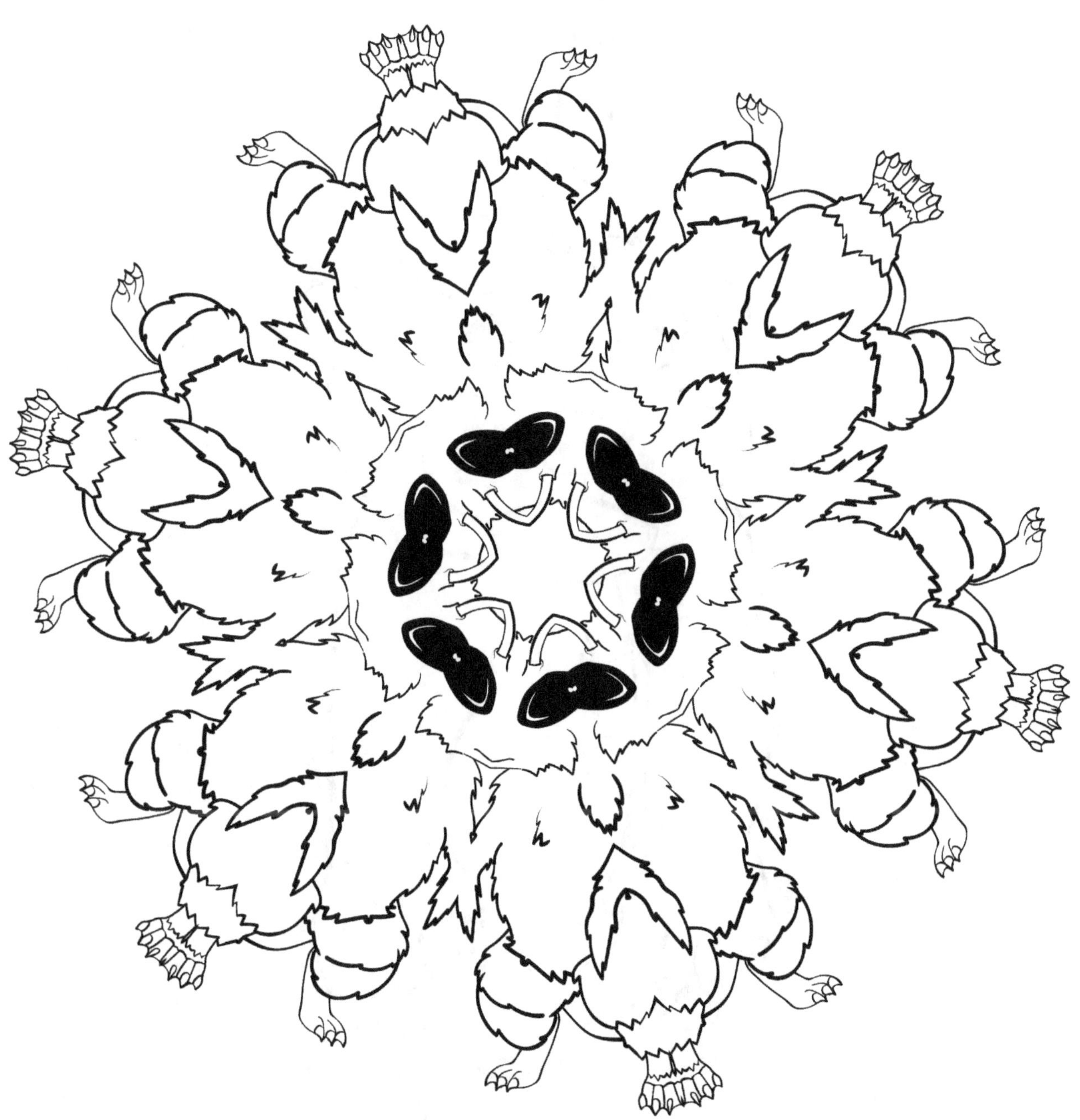

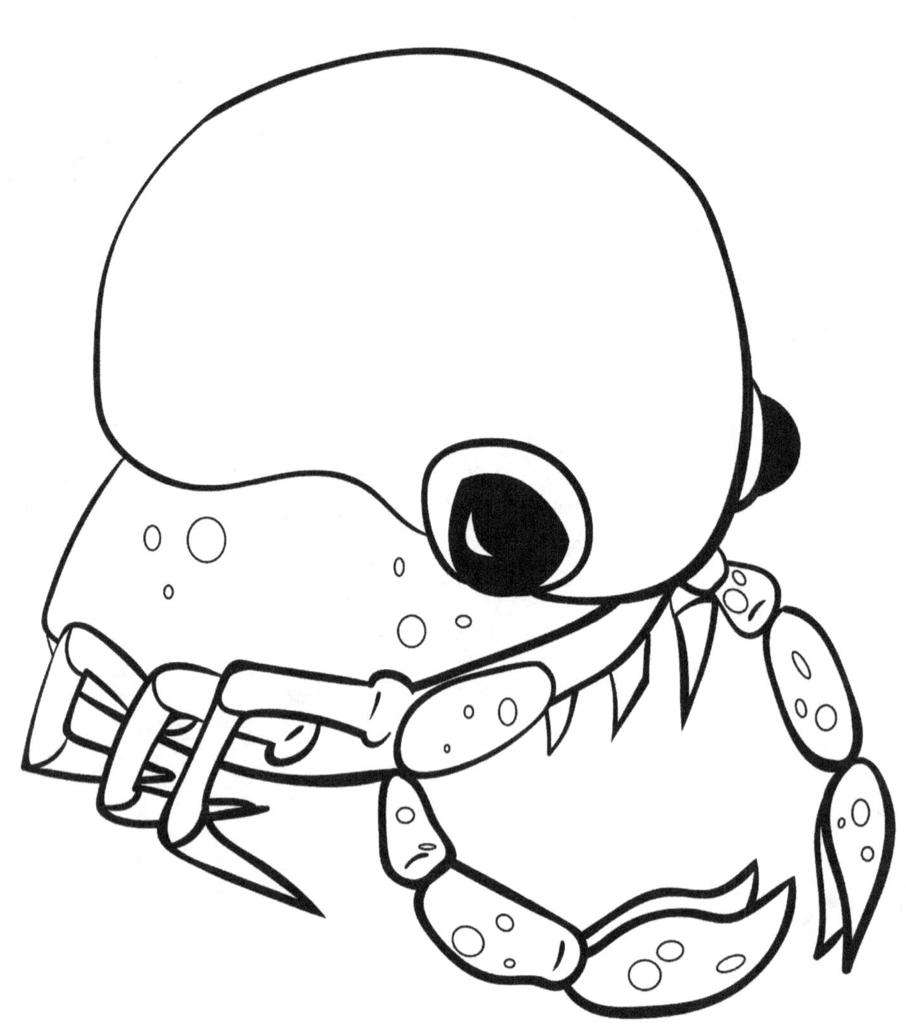

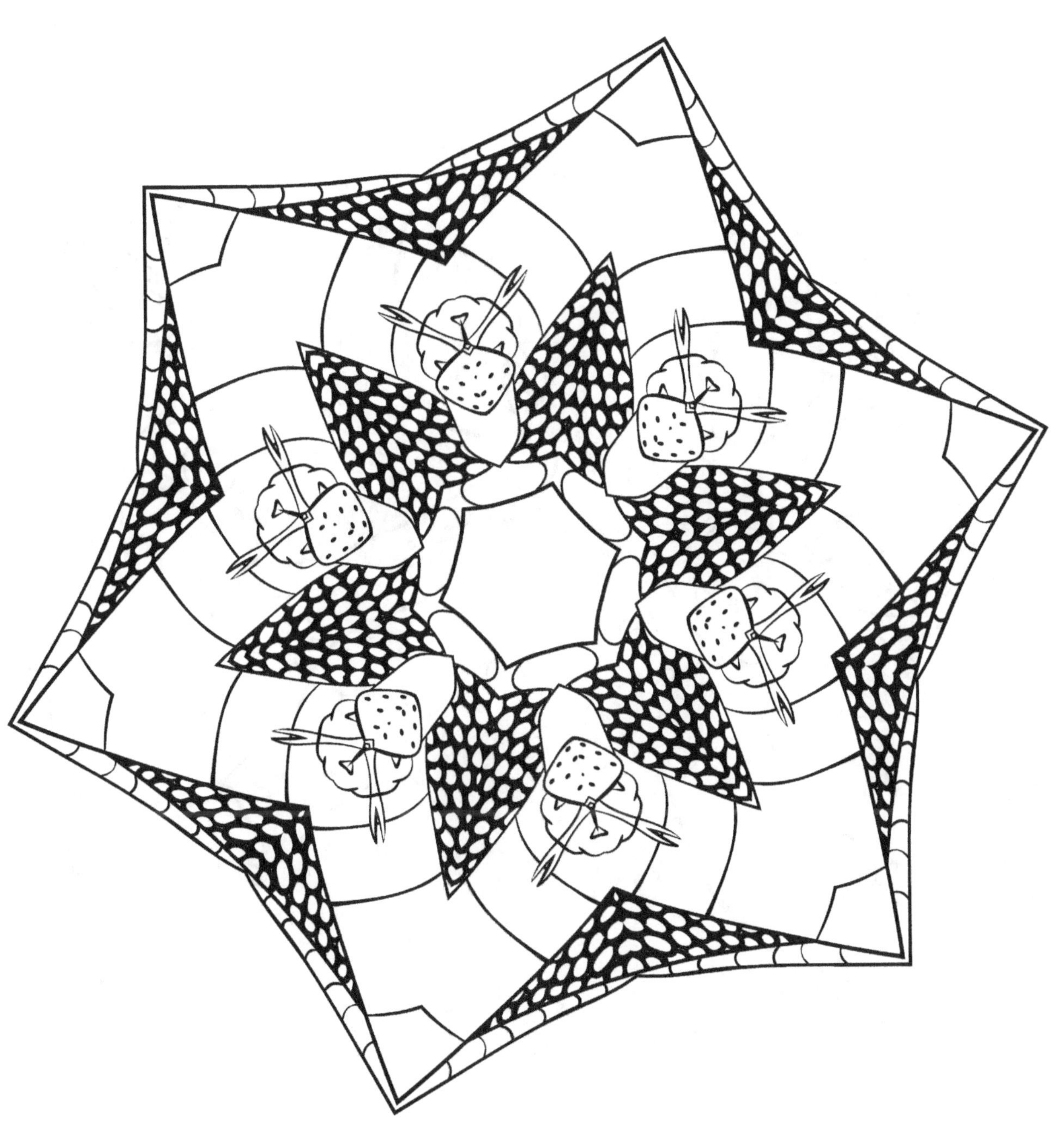

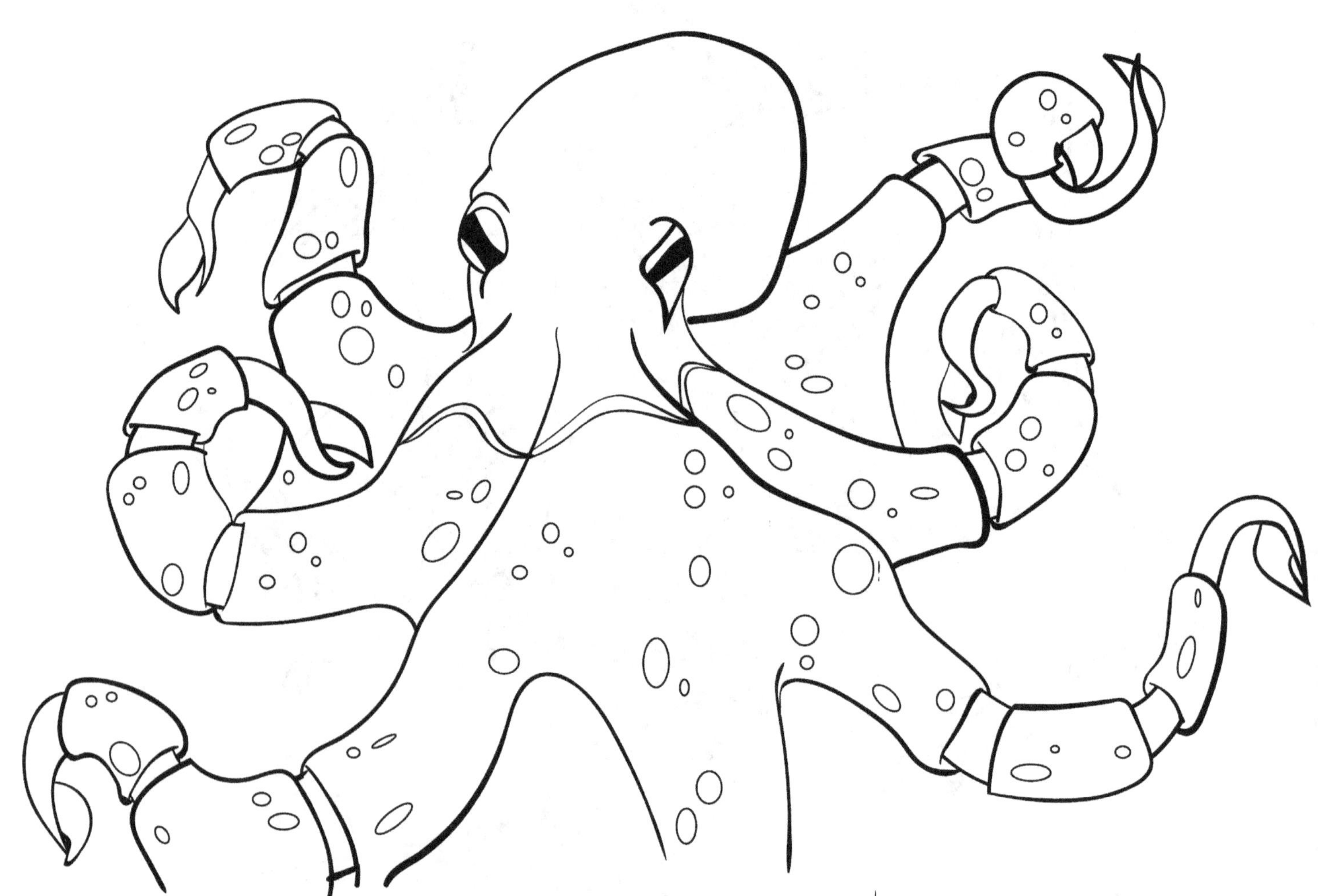

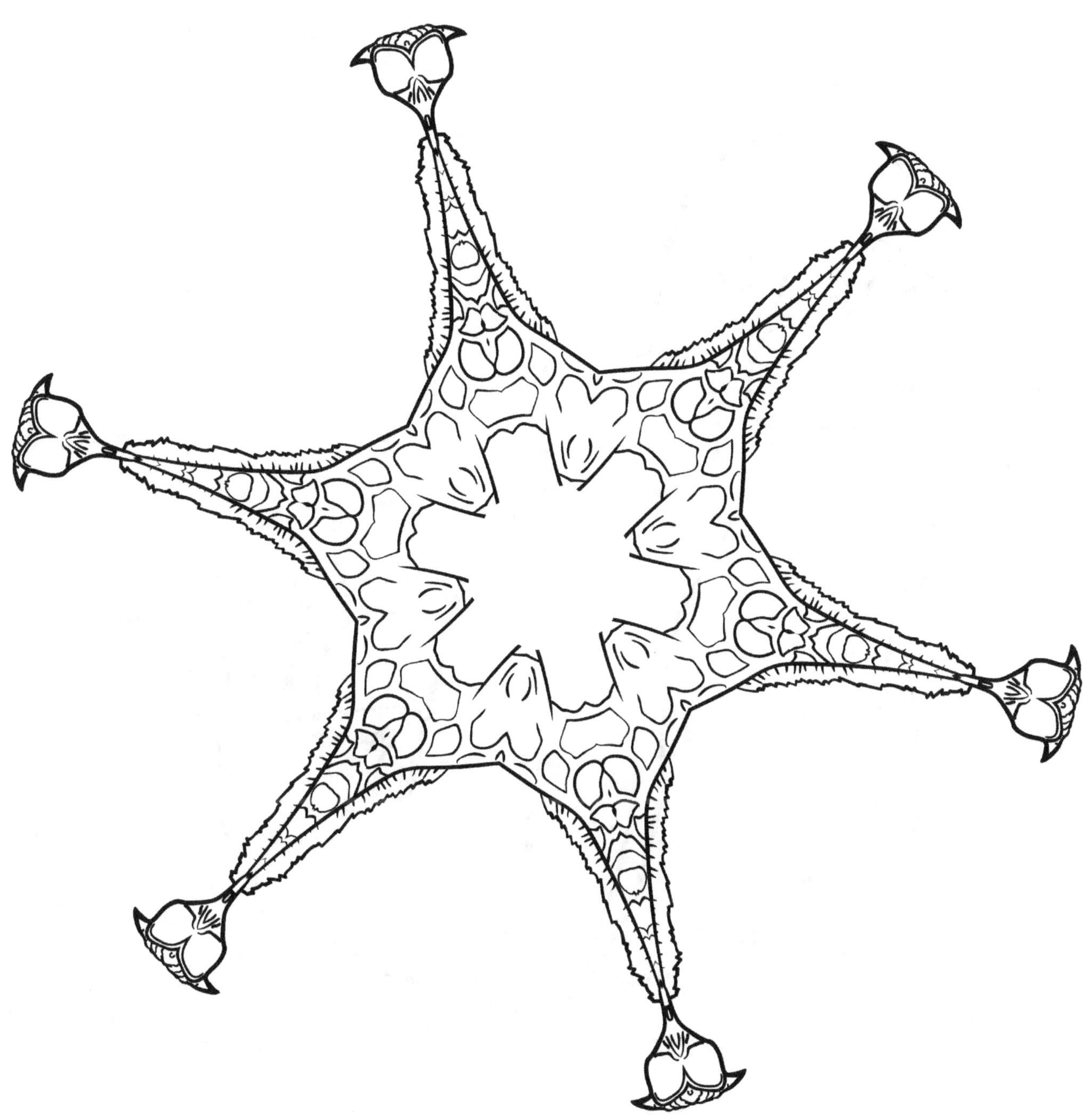

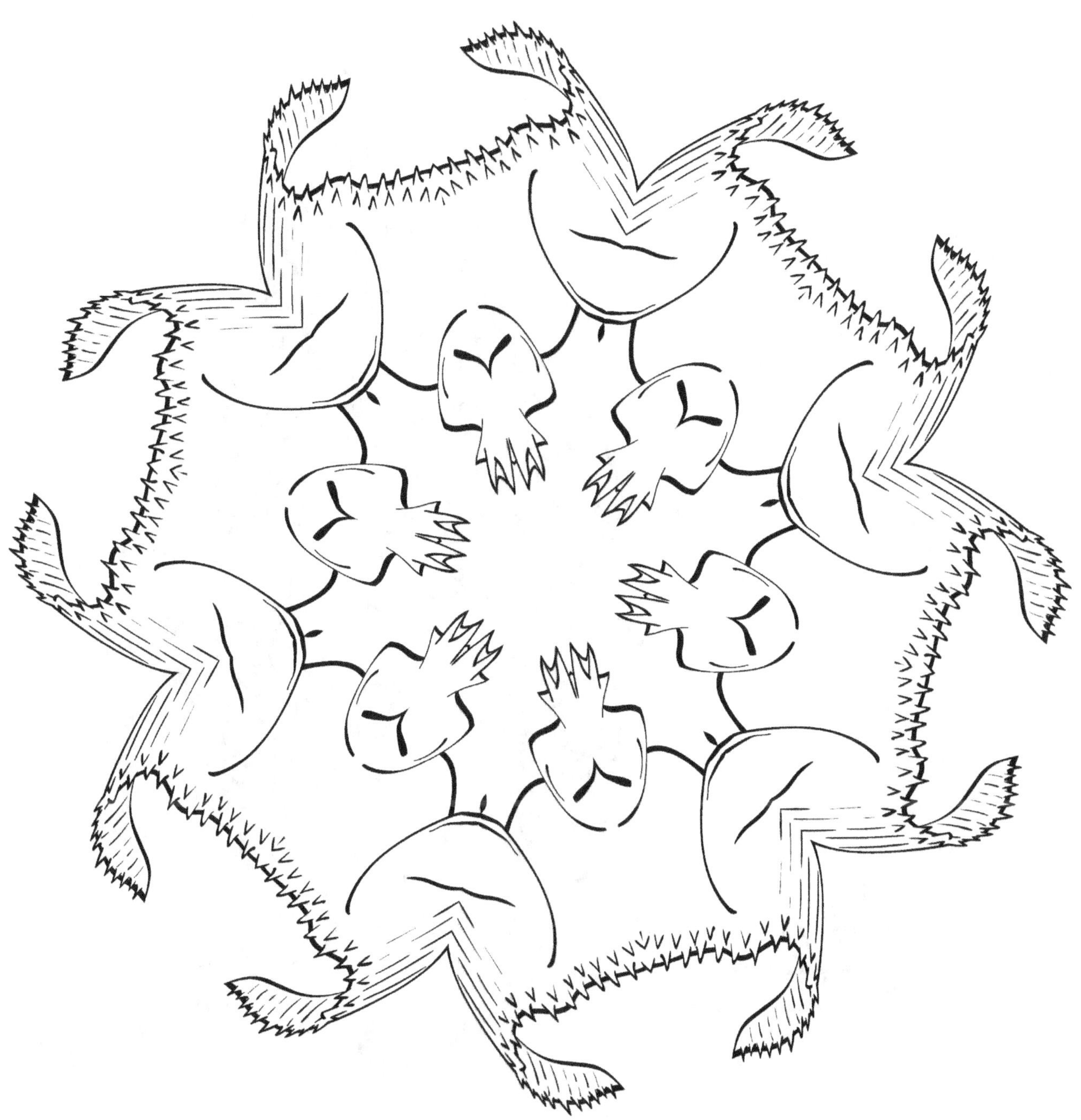

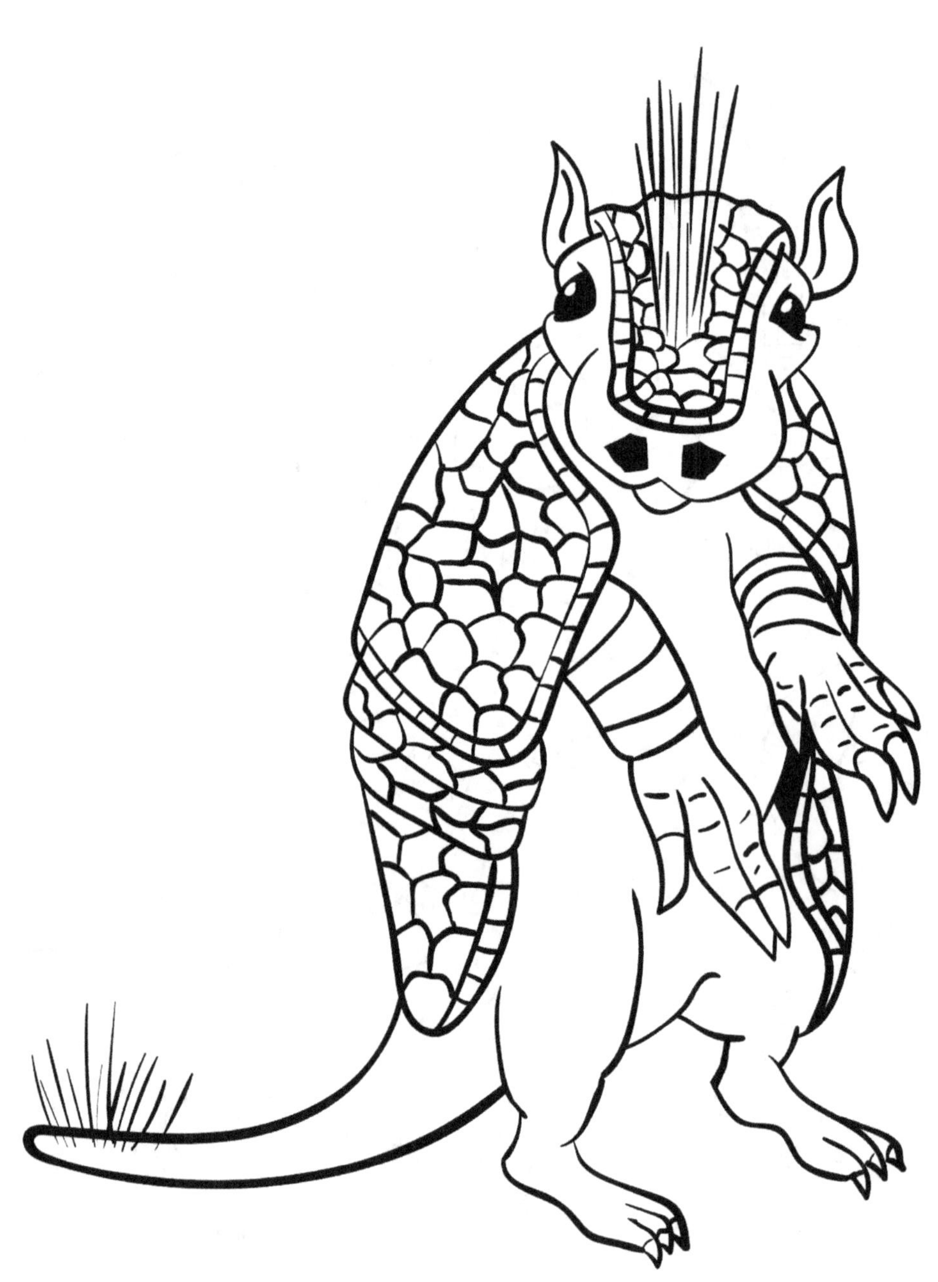

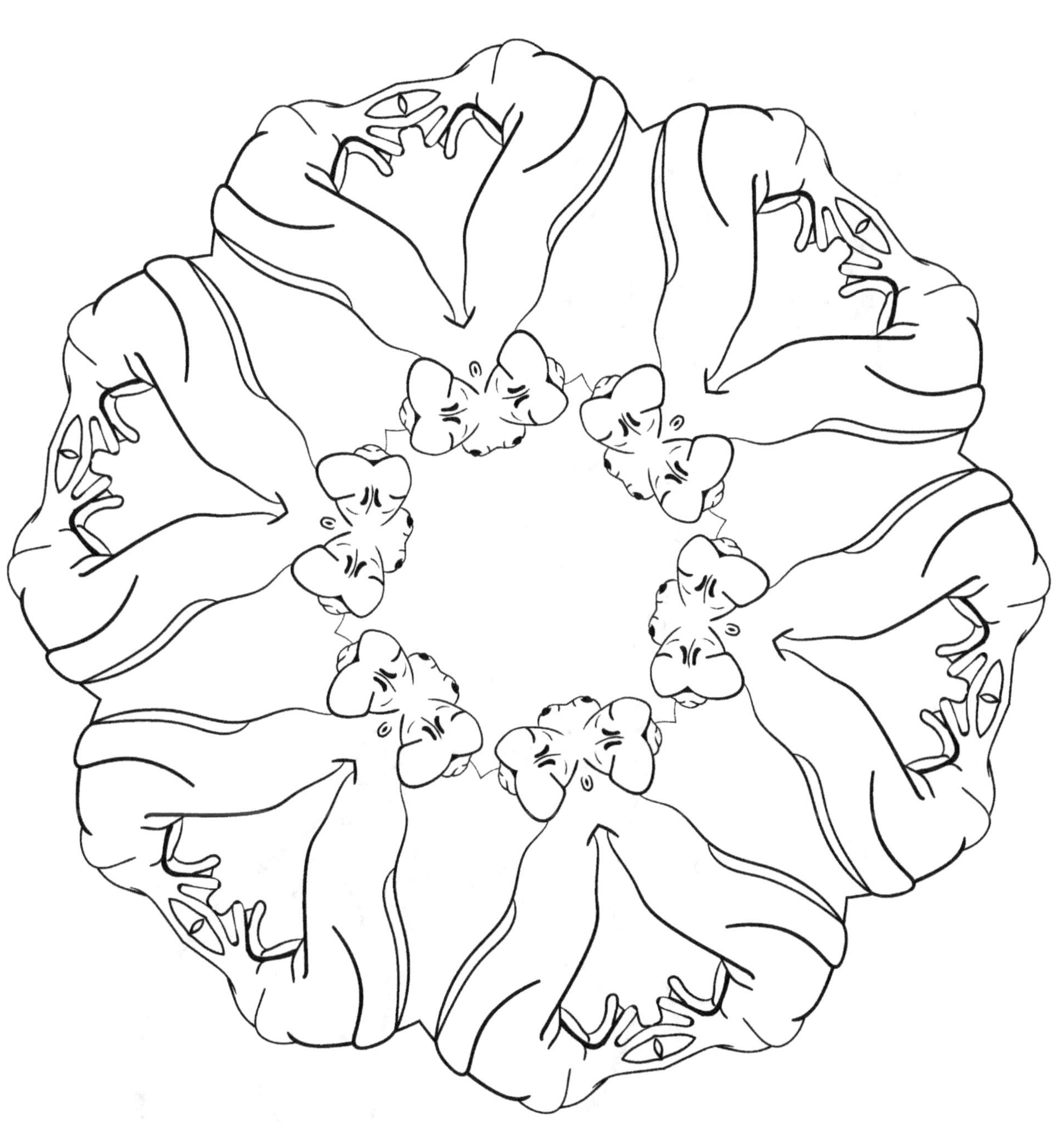

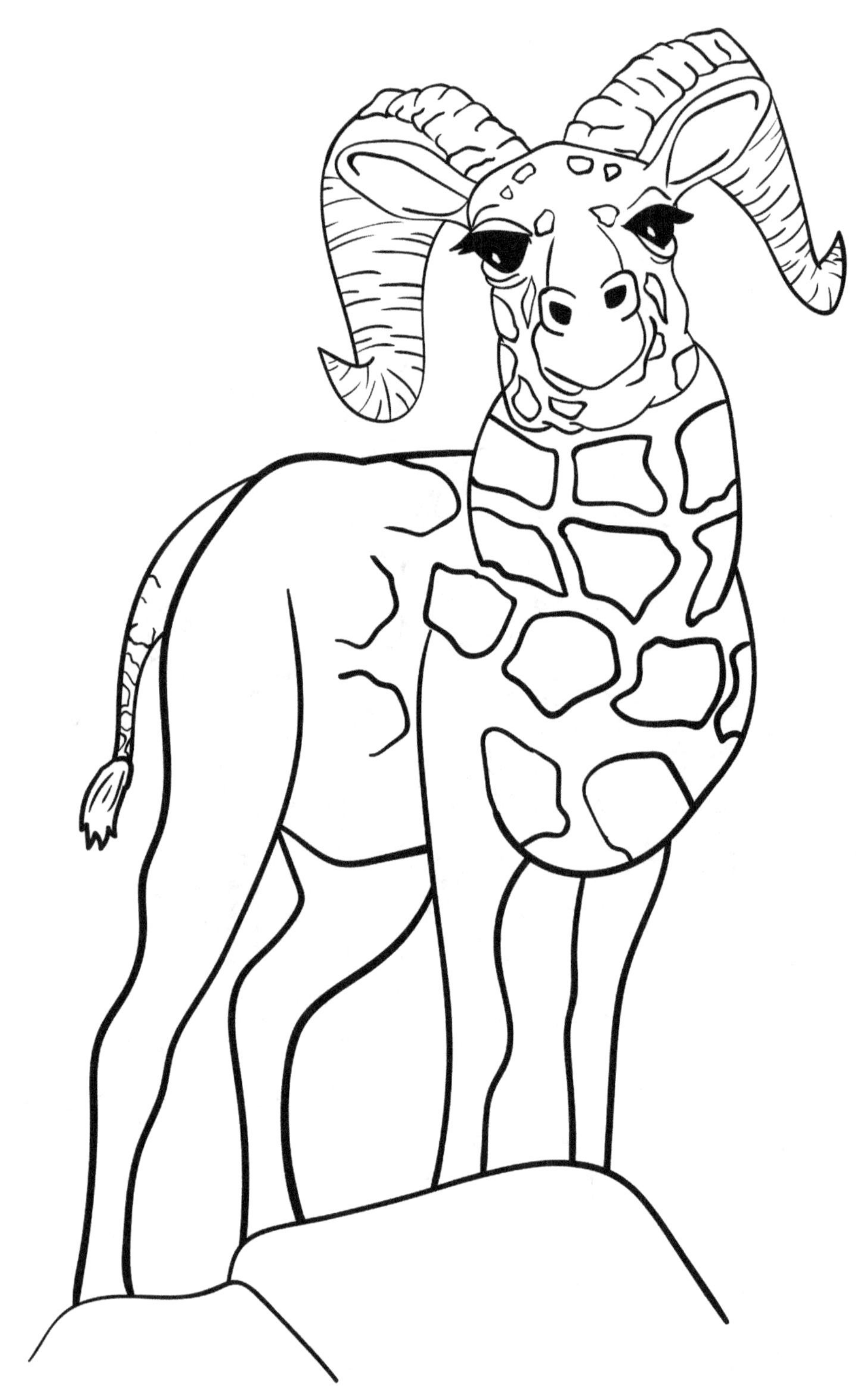

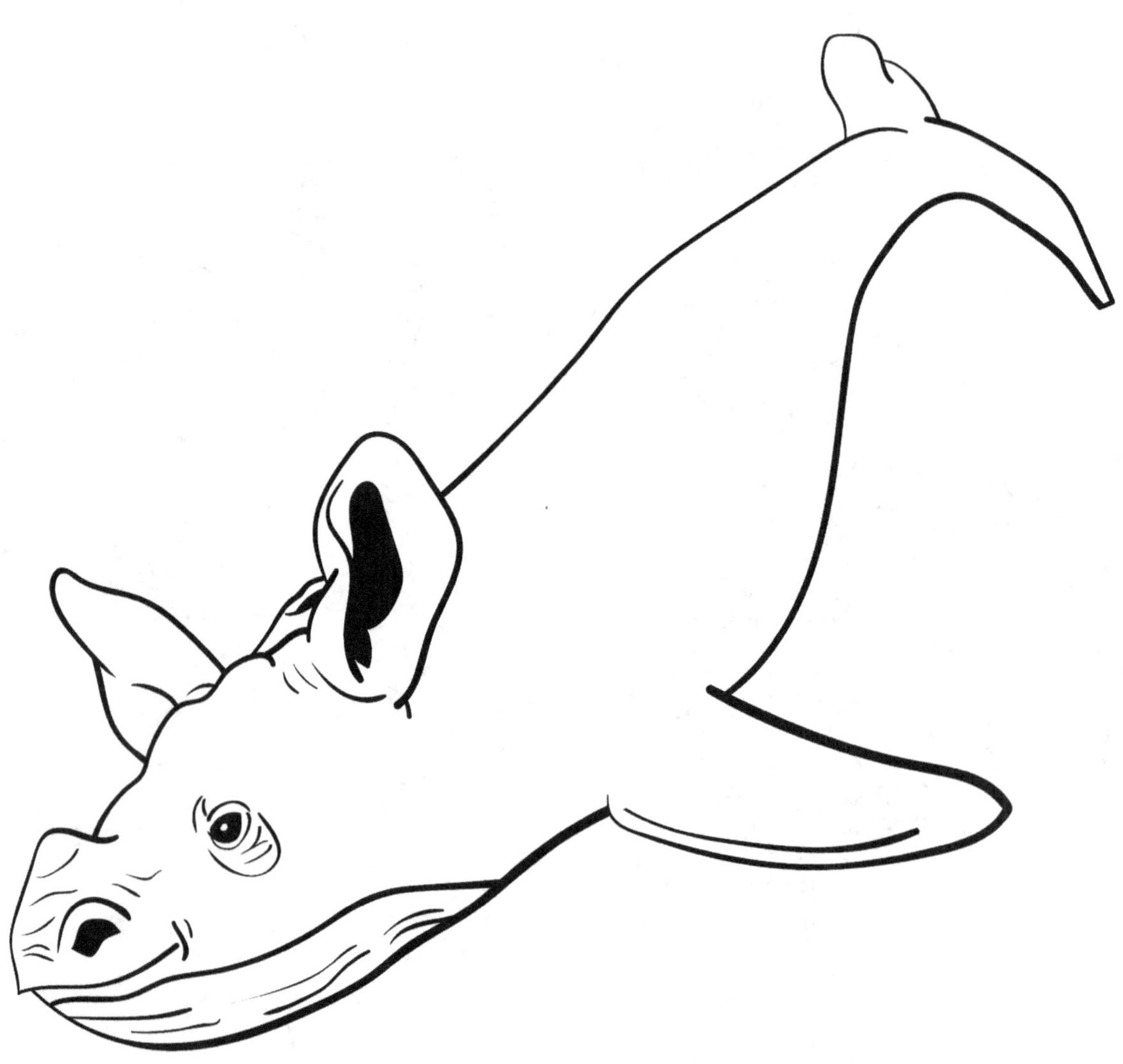

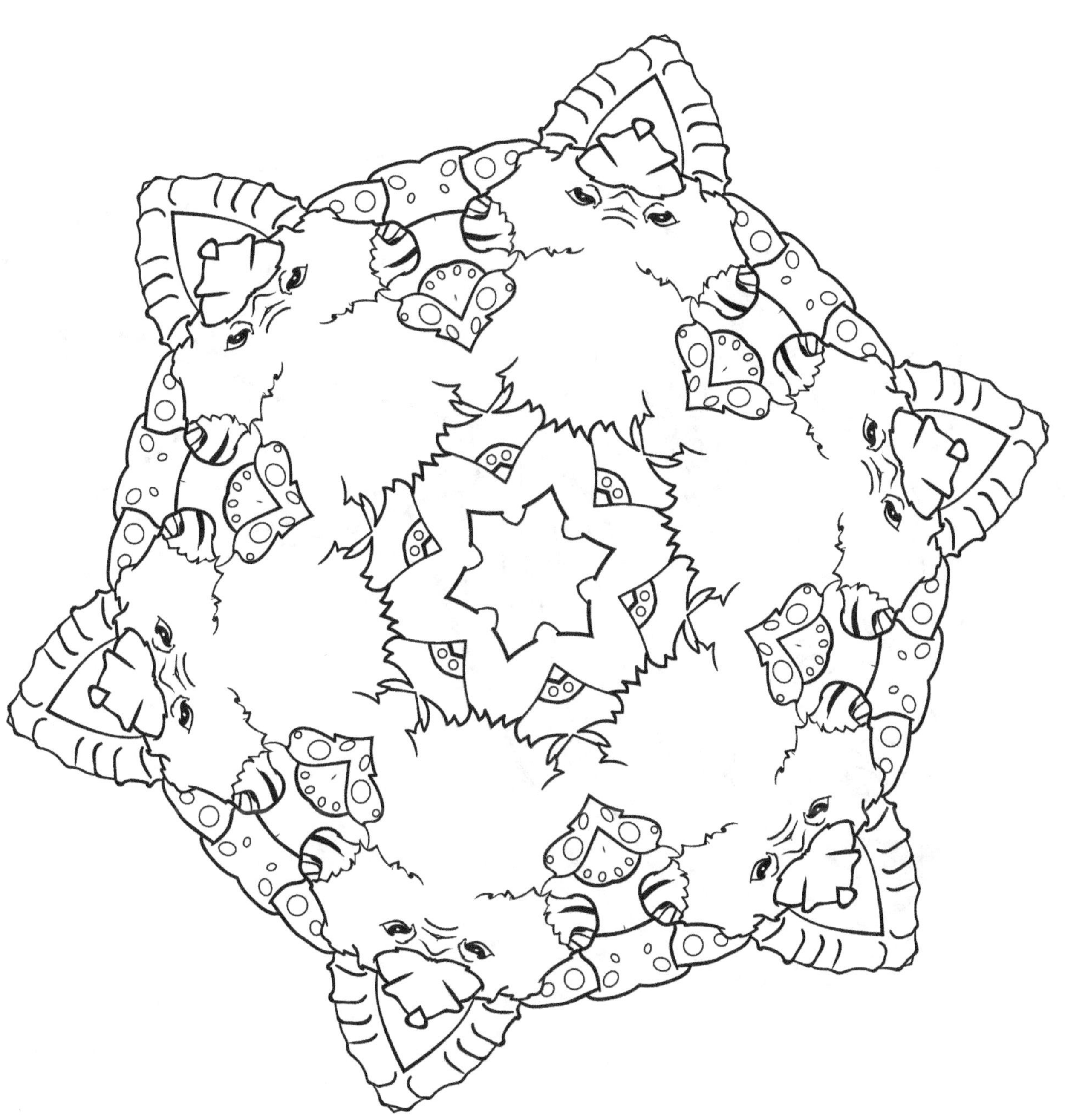

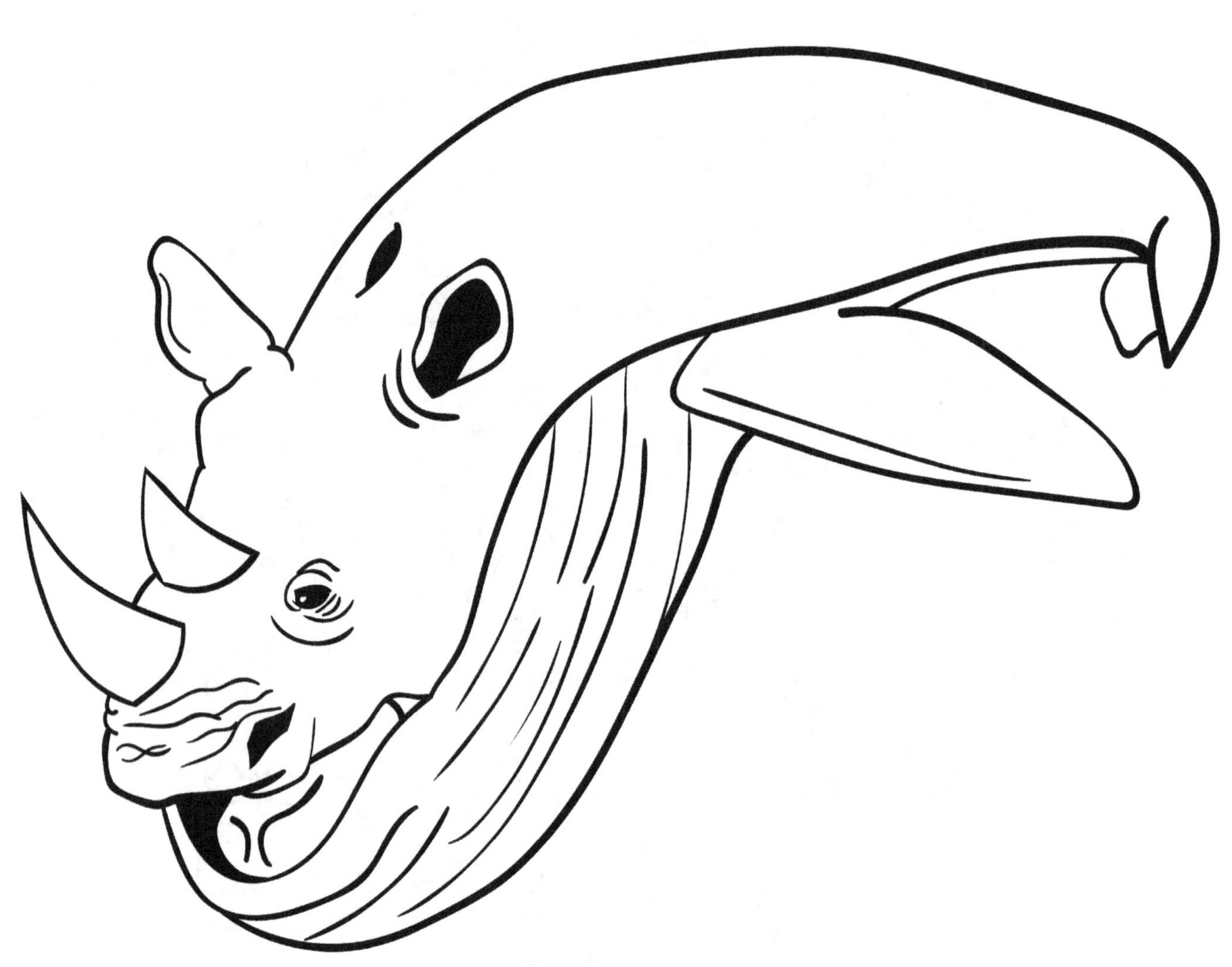

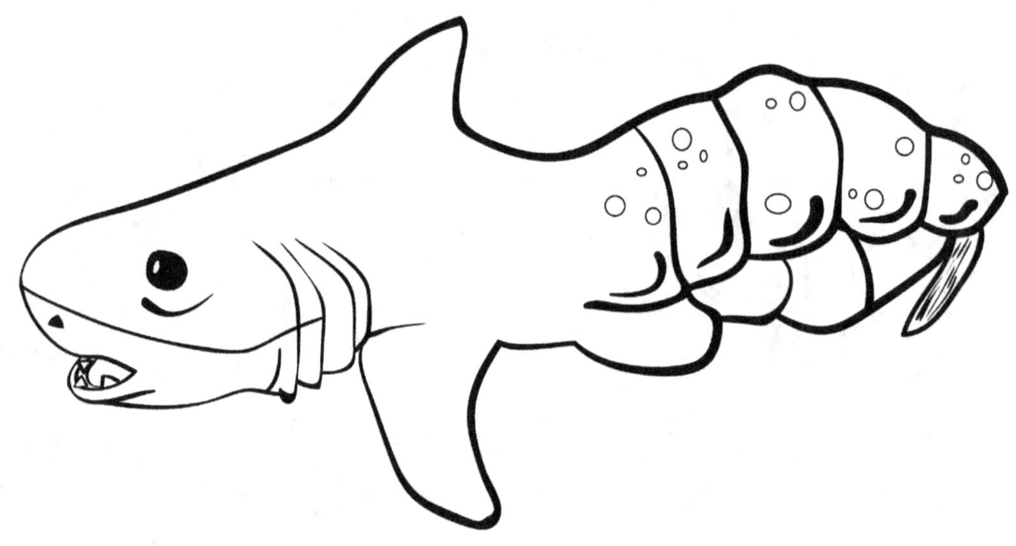

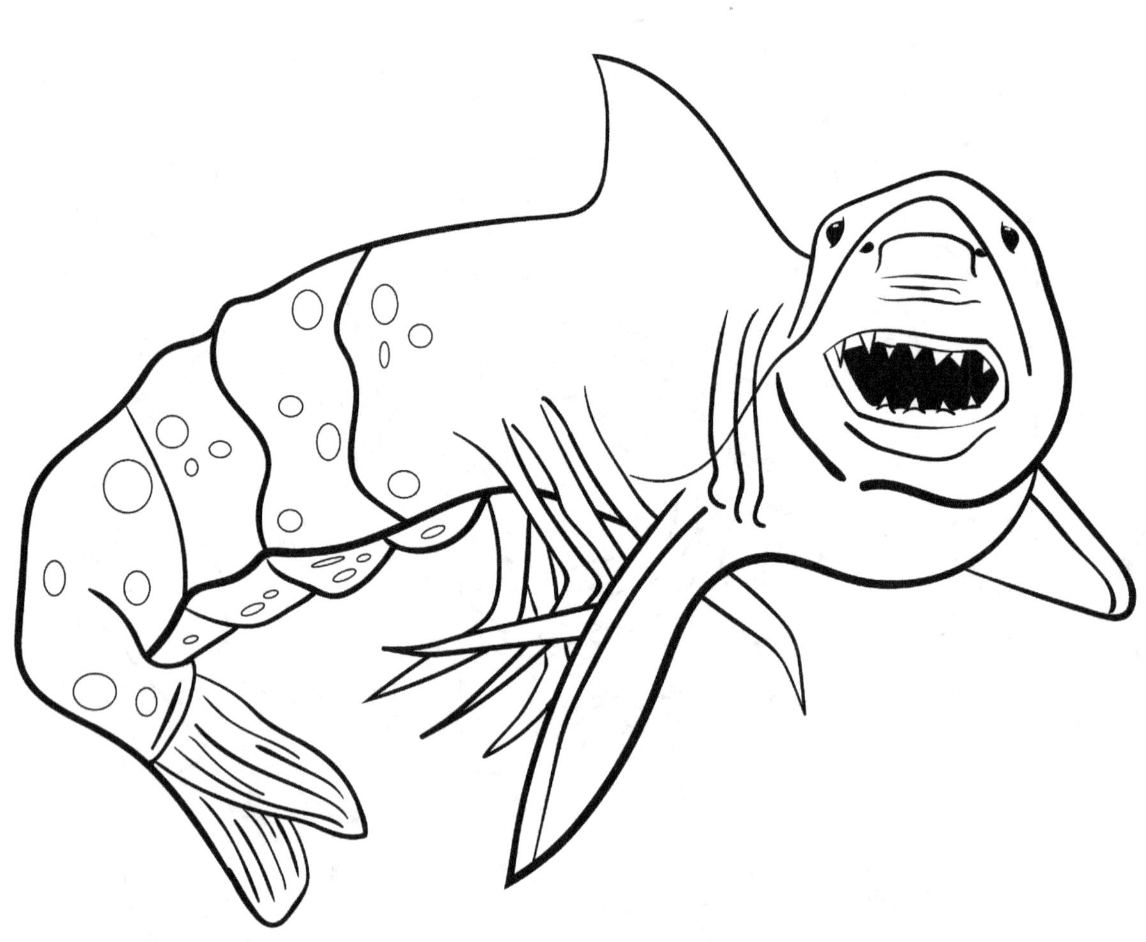

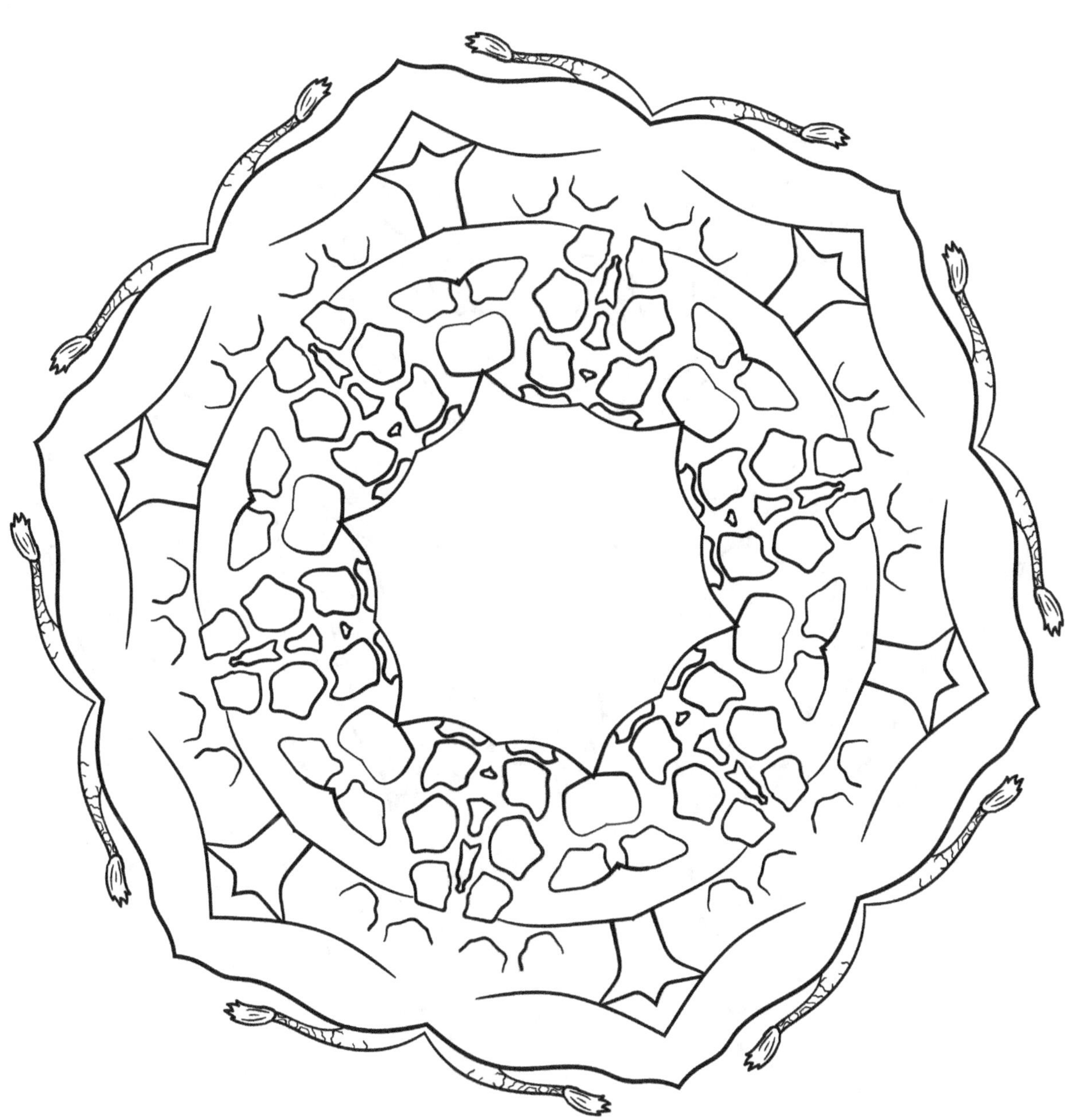

www.ingramcontent.com/pod-product-compliance
Lightning Source LLC
Chambersburg PA
CBHW081243250726
48654CB00012B/1461